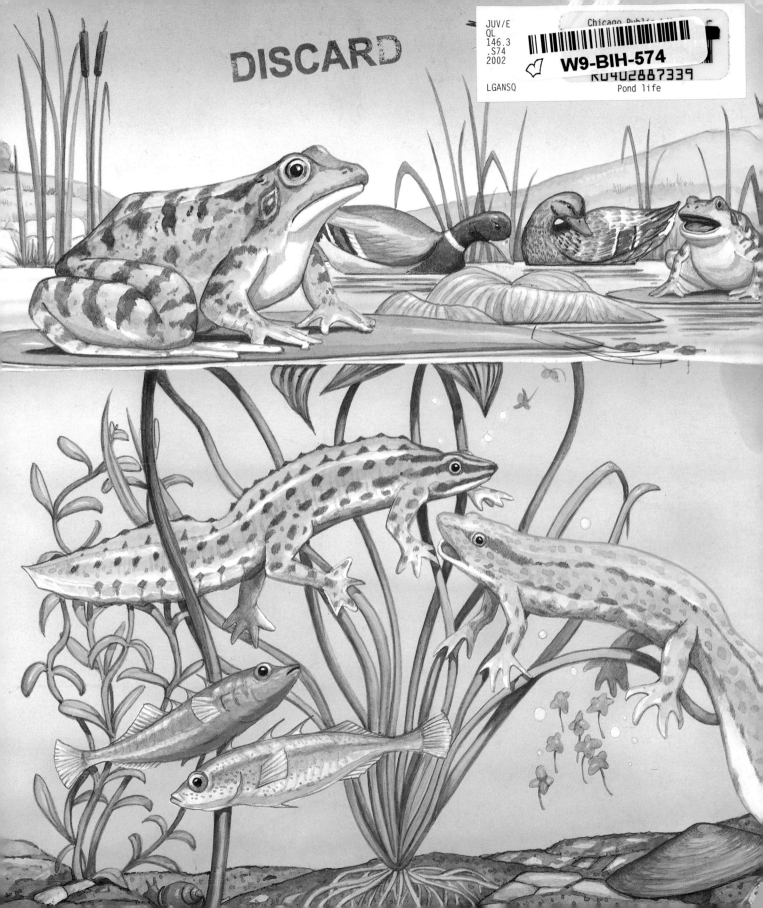

· CYCLES OF LIFE ·
Pond Life

Written by David Stewart
Illustrated by Carolyn Scrace
Created and designed by David Salariya

W
FRANKLIN WATTS
A Division of Scholastic Inc.
NEW YORK • TORONTO • LONDON • AUCKLAND • SYDNEY
MEXICO CITY • NEW DELHI • HONG KONG
DANBURY, CONNECTICUT

Contents

Introduction

Every pond is different. Many of the plants, insects, and animals shown in this book may be found in ponds near you.

Frogs, newts, fish, and some birds live on or in ponds. In this book, you will see how they find mates, how their young are born, and how the young grow into adults.

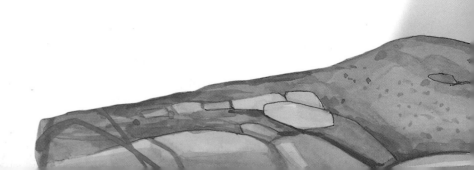

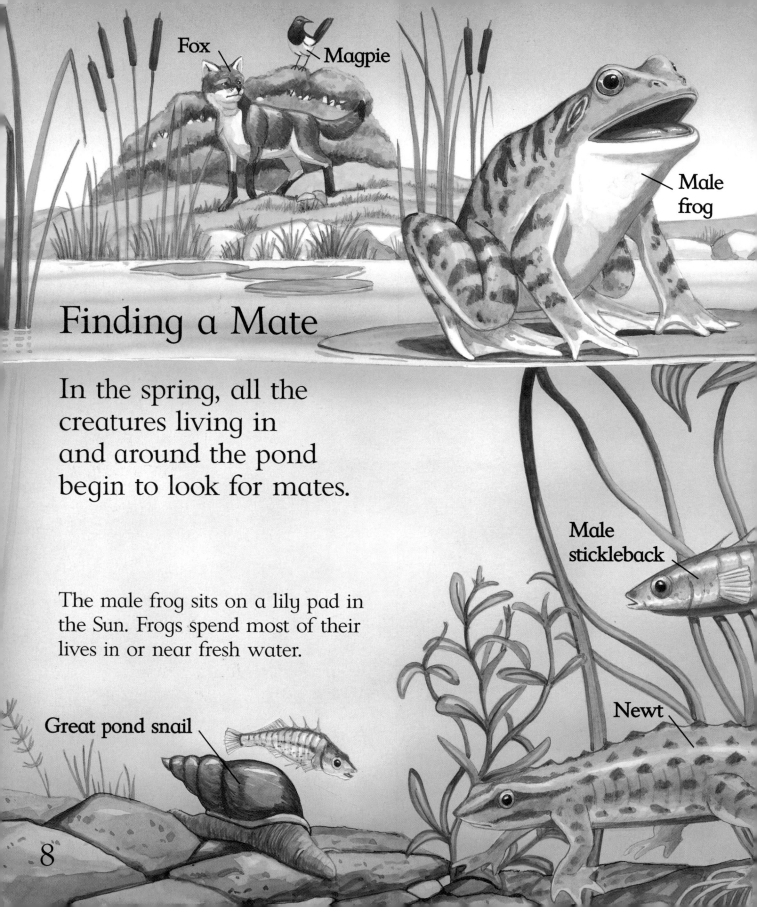

Fox

Magpie

Male frog

Finding a Mate

In the spring, all the
creatures living in
and around the pond
begin to look for mates.

The male frog sits on a lily pad in
the Sun. Frogs spend most of their
lives in or near fresh water.

Male
stickleback

Newt

Great pond snail

Male
duck

Courtship

The stickleback male does a zig-zag dance in the water to attract a female.

The male frog attracts a mate by making his throat swell. Then he croaks loudly. The female answers him in chirps and grunts.

Female
newt

Newts live on land as well as in water. In spring, they enter the water to find a mate. Male and female newts dance before **mating**. This is called **courtship**.

Duckweed

Water louse

11

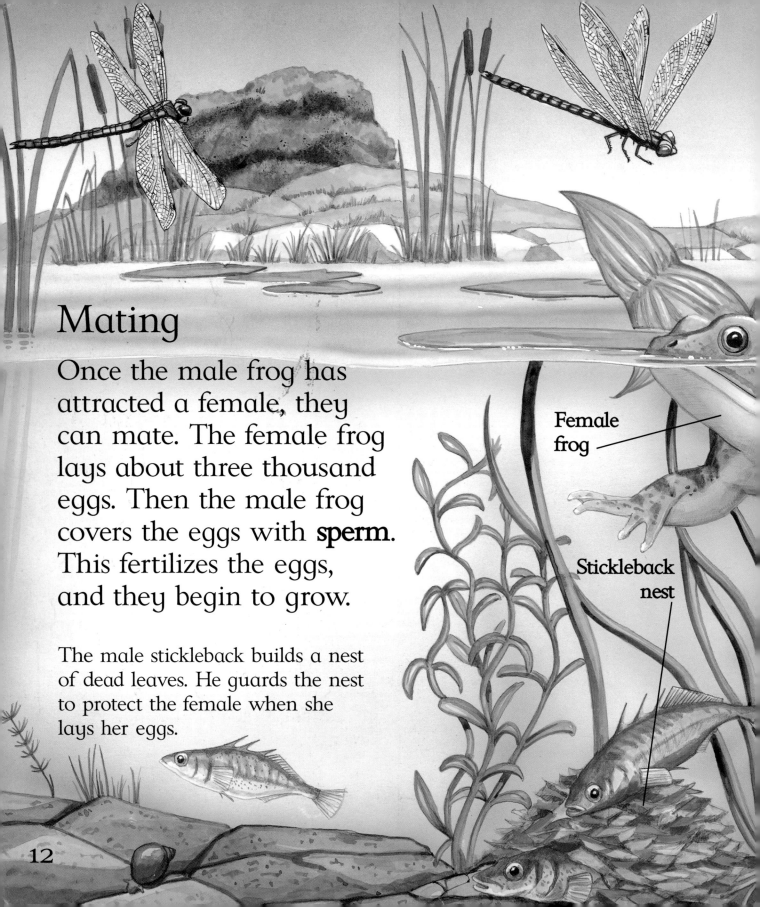

Mating

Once the male frog has attracted a female, they can mate. The female frog lays about three thousand eggs. Then the male frog covers the eggs with **sperm**. This fertilizes the eggs, and they begin to grow.

The male stickleback builds a nest of dead leaves. He guards the nest to protect the female when she lays her eggs.

Female frog

Stickleback nest

Kingfisher

The Eggs Hatch

Dragonfly **nymph**

The fertilized frog's eggs stick together and sink to the bottom of the pond.

Frog spawn

Saucer bug

Tadpole

The jelly around the eggs swells and forms frog spawn. A few days later, **tadpoles hatch** from the eggs.

Pond worm

Tadpoles

Water spider's air bubble

Seven weeks after hatching, the tadpoles still live underwater. They breathe through their **gills** and eat tiny plants.

The tadpoles' back legs start to grow. As they get bigger, tadpoles eat small water animals such as water fleas and pond worms.

Pond worm

Dangerous Times

Great diving beetle

Two weeks later, the tadpoles' gills disappear. The tadpoles then start to breathe using their **lungs**.

Many creatures in the pond like to eat tadpoles. Insects such as the great diving beetle will catch and eat them.

Water scorpion

Tadpoles

Caddis fly

Pond skater

From Tadpoles to Froglets

As spring turns into summer, the tadpoles become young frogs, called **froglets**. They can now swim to the surface of the pond and breathe air. Froglets have long, sticky tongues, good for catching insects.

20

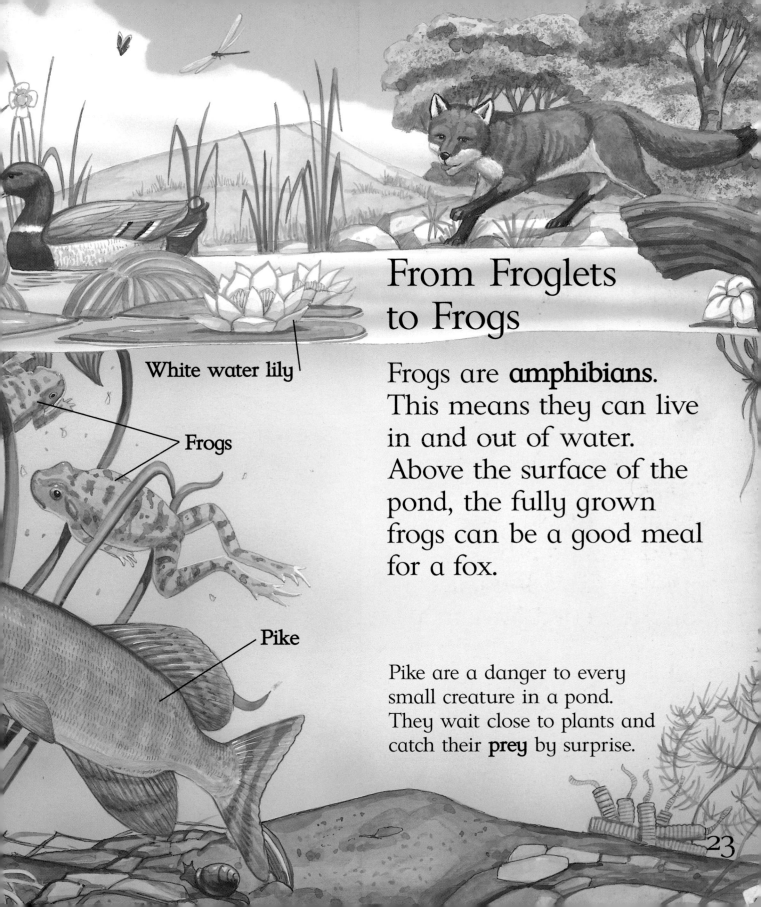

From Froglets to Frogs

White water lily

Frogs

Pike

Frogs are **amphibians**. This means they can live in and out of water. Above the surface of the pond, the fully grown frogs can be a good meal for a fox.

Pike are a danger to every small creature in a pond. They wait close to plants and catch their **prey** by surprise.

23

Autumn Arrives

All the animals born in the spring are now adults. As summer changes to autumn, the weather becomes cooler and wetter. Birds **migrate** to warmer places. Some animals prepare to **hibernate**.

Caddis fly **larva** case

Winter Settles In

Life in the pond is much quieter in winter. Many creatures and plants look dead, but they are not. They are saving their energy for when the warmer weather returns in the spring.

The frog has found a place to hibernate. He will sleep all through winter among the rotting leaves at the bottom of the pond.

Pond Life Through the Year

In spring, the adult frogs look for mates.

Many of the pond animals go through courtship dances to attract a mate.

During mating, the female frog's eggs are fertilized by the male.

Tadpoles hatch from the frog spawn after twenty-one days.

The tadpoles grow into froglets. Their gills disappear, and the froglets breathe with lungs.

By the end of the summer, the froglets have become fully grown frogs. They will soon be looking for mates.

Pond Life Words

Amphibians
Creatures able to live in water or on land. They begin their lives in water.

Courtship
The special things a male creature does to attract a female to be his mate.

Fertilization
When an egg and sperm join together. The egg and sperm will become a baby.

Froglet
A young frog.

Frog spawn
The sticky eggs of a frog that float on the surface of the water. Tadpoles hatch from frog spawn.

Gills
These are needed by animals to breathe underwater. They are outside the body.

Hatch
When a baby creature comes out of its egg.

Hibernate
When an animal sleeps through the winter.

Larva
An insect that has just hatched from its egg.

Lungs
Organs that allow creatures to breathe air.

Mating
The joining of a male (father) with a female (mother) to make babies.

Migrate
To travel a long way, at certain times of the year, to find a warmer place to live.

Nymph
A young dragonfly.

Prey
An animal that is killed by another creature for food.

Sperm
The liquid from the male that joins the egg from the female to produce a baby.

Tadpole
The small creature that hatches from a frog's egg.

Index

Language Consultant: Betty Root
Natural History Consultant: Dr. Gerald Legg

Editors: Karen Barker Smith
Stephanie Cole

Created, designed and produced by
The Salariya Book Company Ltd
Book House
25 Marlborough Place
Brighton BN1 1UB

Visit the Salariya Book Company at
www.salariya.com

A catalog record for this title is available from the Library of Congress.

ISBN 0-531-14660-X (Lib. Bdg.)
ISBN 0-531-14843-2 (Pbk.)

Published in the United States by
Franklin Watts
A Division of Scholastic Inc.
90 Sherman Turnpike
Danbury, CT 06816

Printed in China.